RIVERS OF
NORTH AMERICA

The **Snake** River

by Daniel Gilpin

Gareth Stevens Publishing
A WORLD ALMANAC EDUCATION GROUP COMPANY

Please visit our web site at: www.garethstevens.com
For a free color catalog describing Gareth Stevens Publishing's list of high-quality
books and multimedia programs, call 1-800-542-2595 (USA) or 1-800-387-3178
(Canada). Gareth Stevens Publishing's fax: (414) 332-3567.

Library of Congress Cataloging-in-Publication Data

Gilpin, Daniel.
    The Snake River / by Daniel Gilpin.
       p. cm. — (Rivers of North America)
    Includes bibliographical references and index.
    Contents: A wild river—From source to mouth—The life of the river—Exploring new lands—The
frontier river—Places to visit—How rivers form.
    ISBN 0-8368-3761-4 (lib. bdg.)
    1. Snake River (Wyo.-Wash.)—Juvenile literature. [1. Snake River (Wyo.-Wash.).]
I. Title. II. Series.
F752.S7G555 2003
979.6'1—dc21   2003042743

This North American edition first published in 2004 by
Gareth Stevens Publishing
A World Almanac Education Group Company
330 West Olive Street, Suite 100
Milwaukee, Wisconsin 53212 USA

Original copyright © 2004 The Brown Reference Group plc. This U.S. edition copyright © 2004
by Gareth Stevens, Inc.

Author: Daniel Gilpin
Editor: Tom Jackson
Consultant: Judy Wheatley Maben, Education Director, Water Education Foundation
Designer: Steve Wilson
Cartographer: Mark Walker
Picture Researcher: Clare Newman
Indexer: Kay Ollerenshaw
Managing Editor: Bridget Giles
Art Director: Dave Goodman

Gareth Stevens Editor: Betsy Rasmussen
Gareth Stevens Designer: Melissa Valuch

Picture Credits: Cover: The Snake River passing the Grand Teton Range, Wyoming. (NHPA: John Shaw)
Contents: Snake River at Thousand Springs, Idaho.

Key: l–left, r–right, t–top, b–bottom.
Corbis: Peter Beck 27; Bettmann 18t, 18/19, 23t; Philip James Corwin 29b; Ric Ergenbright 4b; Raymond
Gehman 15b; Kevin R. Morris 17; Pierre Perrin 21; Michael T. Sedam 4/5; Karl Weatherly 23b; Robert
Young Pelton 24; Getty Images: 14, 16; Idaho Division of Tourism: Idaho Department of Commerce 5r, 7b,
8/9b, 8/9t, 20, 25, 29t; NASA: 9r; PhotoDisc: Alan & Sandy Carey 12; StockTrek 11b; John Wang 7t; Still
Pictures: Peter Arnold/Jeff & Alexa Henry 28; Peter Arnold/S. J. Krasemann 10; Peter Arnold/Alan
Majchrowicz 22; Peter Arnold/Lynda Richardson 11t; U.S. Army Corps of Engineers: 13t, 13b, 26; Werner
Forman Archive: H. W. Read Collection, Plains Indian Museum, B. Bill Hist. Center, Cody, Wyoming 15t

Printed in the United States of America

1 2 3 4 5 6 7 8 9 07 06 05 04 03

Table of Contents

A Wild River

The Snake River flows past some of the most breathtaking natural features in the United States. Pioneers followed the river on their way west, and today it supplies a thriving farming industry.

Left: *Tourists paddle through rapids on the Snake River in Wyoming.*

The Snake River has earned a place in North American history. Native people had been living beside the river for thousands of years when U.S. explorers Meriwether Lewis and William Clark traveled down it in 1805. Later, the Snake became part of the Oregon Trail, a route to the west that pioneers followed, hoping to build new lives for themselves in the Pacific Northwest.

Spectacular Journey

Beginning in Yellowstone National Park and flowing in a great loop through the Rocky Mountains, the Snake River is one of the nation's

Right: *The Snake River flows past the city of Idaho Falls, Idaho. The city takes its name from a waterfall on the river.*

Below: *The river's water tumbles over the mighty Shoshone Falls near the city of Twin Falls, Idaho. Shoshone Falls is the largest set of waterfalls on the Snake River.*

most beautiful rivers. At the start of its journey, the river cuts through the spectacular Teton Range. Farther downstream, the river dives over Shoshone Falls—1000 feet (304 meters) wide and higher than Niagara Falls—before entering Hells Canyon, the deepest gorge in the United States.

From source to mouth, the flow of the Snake goes through changes. In some places it is wild and thunders over fierce rapids. In other areas, the river slowly twists and turns. Near its end, the river grows sluggish, as it flows over flat land between dams to join the Columbia River in southeastern Washington.

Supplying People

As well as being a great physical force, the Snake River is also a vital part of the lives of the people who live along its banks. The river waters crops in some of the richest farming land in the country and supplies homes and businesses in nearby towns and cities. Dams along the river generate large amounts of electricity, and the lower section of the river is a wide highway for cargo barges and other boats.

The Snake River also provides many opportunities for having fun. Rafters and kayakers flock to the river to test themselves on its impressive rapids, and fishers try to catch the river's fish. The river's scenery also draws tourists to it from all over the world.

1 From Source to Mouth

From the awesome natural beauty of Yellowstone National Park to tall waterfalls and deep canyons, a journey down the Snake River is certainly a wild ride.

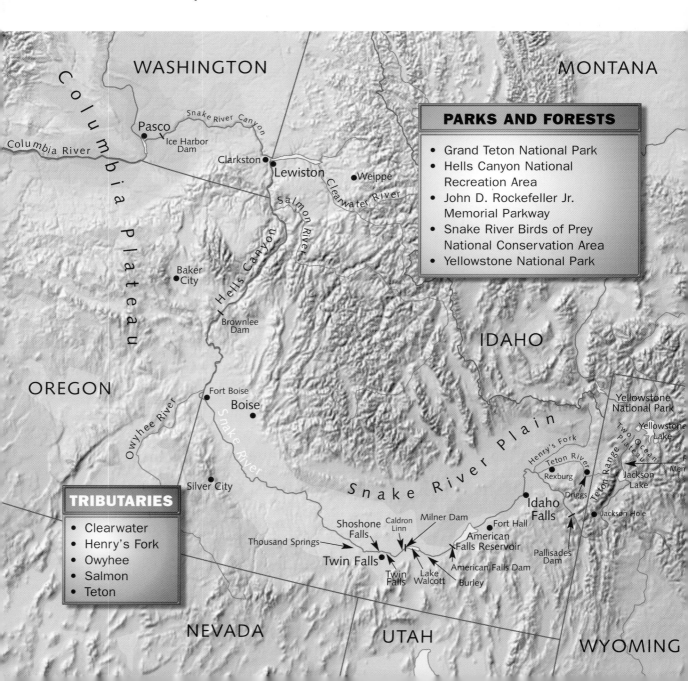

WASHINGTON

MONTANA

Columbia River

Columbia Plateau

Pasco

Snake River Canyon

Ice Harbor Dam

Clarkston

Lewiston

Weippe

Clearwater River

Salmon River

Hells Canyon

Baker City

Brownlee Dam

PARKS AND FORESTS

- Grand Teton National Park
- Hells Canyon National Recreation Area
- John D. Rockefeller Jr. Memorial Parkway
- Snake River Birds of Prey National Conservation Area
- Yellowstone National Park

IDAHO

OREGON

Owyhee River

Fort Boise

Boise

Snake River

Silver City

Snake River Plain

Henry's Fork

Teton River

Rexburg

Driggs

Yellowstone National Park

Two Ocean Plateau

Yellowstone Lake

Jackson Lake

Teton Range

Jackson Hole

Idaho Falls

TRIBUTARIES

- Clearwater
- Henry's Fork
- Owyhee
- Salmon
- Teton

Thousand Springs

Shoshone Falls

Caldron Linn

Milner Dam

Fort Hall

American Falls Reservoir

Pallisades Dam

Twin Falls

Twin Falls

Lake Walcott

American Falls Dam

Burley

NEVADA

UTAH

WYOMING

The Snake River flows past some of the most amazing scenery in North America. Its source is on the Two Ocean Plateau in Yellowstone National Park in Wyoming—the oldest national park in the United States. From there it flows 1,038 miles (1,670 kilometers) through Idaho, joining the Columbia River in southeastern Washington. The river carries water draining from a much wider area, including parts of Nevada, Oregon, and Utah.

Above: *The tall peaks of the Grand Tetons are reflected in the water of the Snake River.*

Two Miles High

From the first tiny trickle, the Snake River crisscrosses with many other channels, becoming a small stream that runs across Two Oceans Plateau. Still 2 miles (3.2 km) above sea level, it winds 42 miles (67.5 km) to the edge

Right: *Water plunges over Mesa Falls on Henry's Fork, a tributary of the Snake River in eastern Idaho.*

KEY FACTS	
Length:	1,038 miles (1,670 km)
Drainage basin:	110,900 square miles (287,200 sq km)
Source:	Yellowstone National Park, Wyoming
Mouth:	Columbia River near Pasco, Washington
Natural features:	Shoshone Falls, Hells Canyon
Economic uses:	Irrigation, hydroelectricity, transportation
Major dams:	Palisades Dam, American Falls Dam, Milner Dam, Brownlee Dam, Ice Harbor Dam
Major cities:	Idaho Falls, Boise, and Lewiston, Idaho; and Pasco, Washington

of Yellowstone, then flows through the John D. Rockefeller Jr. Memorial Parkway into Jackson Lake and Grand Teton National Park. Jackson Lake is fed by several smaller creeks, and by the time it leaves the lake, the Snake River has grown into a broad flow.

Forty miles (64 km) downstream, the Snake River crosses the border from Wyoming into Idaho and pours into the Palisades Reservoir, held back by the

Palisades Dam—the first dam on the river's journey. From here, the Snake runs beneath rugged mountains to the eastern edge of the Snake River Plain. There, it is joined by the Teton River and Henry's Fork, a river fed by hot springs 60 miles (96 km) away in the mountains west of Yellowstone.

Onto the Plain

The grasslands and forests of the Snake River Plain reach halfway across Idaho. Along the plain, the river drops over three spectacular waterfalls. The first, Idaho Falls, is 30 miles (48 km) south of the river's junction with Henry's Fork. Today, there is a city built around and named for the Idaho Falls. Although not high, the beautiful falls can be seen from the nearby highway.

Farther downstream, the Snake River rushes into the American Falls Reservoir. Despite its name, the reservoir has no waterfalls linked to it, apart from the artificial one formed by water pouring over the dam at its southern end. From there, the river runs toward the relatively new Milner Dam. Rebuilt in 1992, it crosses the Snake near the town of Burley.

Downstream from the Milner Dam, the river runs through steep-sided canyons until it reaches two waterfalls—Twin Falls and the enormous Shoshone Falls farther west. At Twin Falls, the Snake River drops 135 feet (41 m). These falls are dwarfed by Shoshone Falls, however, which at 212 feet (65 m) are taller than those at Niagara.

Above: *The Snake River flows between the craggy cliffs of Hells Canyon.*

Below: *Water flows out from the Snake River Plain at Thousand Springs.*

Above right: *A picture taken by a satellite looking south shows the Snake River flowing through Washington before joining the Columbia River.*

Mountain Channel

Not far from Shoshone Falls, the Snake River runs onto the Columbia Plateau. There, it flows into a small reservoir, created by the dam at the Swan Falls power plant. A little way downstream, the Owyhee River meets the Snake, and from that point, the Snake forms the border between Idaho and Oregon.

As it flows northward along the border, the Snake enters Hells Canyon, the deepest canyon in the United States—more than one mile (1.6 km) deep in some places. There, the river encounters three more dams before reaching the northern end of the canyon and meeting with the wild Salmon River. The Salmon is also known as the "River of No Return" because of its fierce current and terrible rapids. Soon after that point, the Snake forms Idaho's border with Washington for about 30 miles (48 km).

At Clarkston, Washington, the Clearwater River meets the Snake. Then, the Snake turns west, heading into Washington. The surrounding hills become less steep, and the river slows a little as it heads through the state's drier, more barren land.

A few miles from the border, the river flows beneath the 2,000-foot (610-m) cliffs of the Snake River Canyon. Close to the city of Pasco, Washington, the Snake pours into the Columbia River, which flows through the Cascade Mountains and past Portland, Oregon, to the Pacific Ocean.

2 The Life of the River

The Snake River passes through plenty of untouched wilderness that provides refuge for many interesting animals, including elk, moose, bears, wolves, sheep, goats, and falcons.

The Snake River winds through some of the wildest country in the United States. It starts life in the untouched wilderness of Yellowstone National Park, twisting between the peaks of the Teton Mountains, and crossing the Snake River Plain and Columbia Plateau, before reaching the dry scrublands of Washington.

Forest Slopes

On its route, the river passes through many preserves and conservation areas. It is fed by tributaries that are rarely traveled by people, such as the Salmon River. For its first 100 miles (160 km), the river winds through the mountains and is surrounded by rock-covered slopes, alpine meadows, and thick pine forests.

Grizzly bears and timber wolves, which were wiped out from much of the territory earlier, are now common there, having been reintroduced to the area. The wolves hunt wild bison, moose, mule deer, and white-tailed deer in the forests. Mountain lions stalk bighorn sheep and Rocky Mountain goats on the open slopes higher up. Smaller mammals include coyotes, foxes, and marten. In

Below: *A prairie falcon stands high on a cliff above the Snake River in Idaho. Many birds of prey live in a nature preserve beside the river.*

BEAVERS OF THE TETONS

The creeks and streams that feed the Snake River in the Teton Mountains are prime habitat for beavers (right). Beavers spend a lot of time in water. They create large ponds in which to live by damming rivers and streams. In spring and summer, they feed on leaves, ferns, grasses, and water plants, but in fall and winter, they eat mostly wood. Beavers spend the winter with their families inside lodges, built in the center of their ponds. They feed on bark and other woody material collected in the fall and stored underwater. Because the entrances and exits to their lodges are below the water surface, beavers can retrieve stored food even when their ponds have frozen over.

addition, countless birds live there—more than three hundred species of birds live in the area of Yellowstone alone.

Near its source, the Snake River has a different group of inhabitants. Otters hunt river fish, and beavers dam streams that run into the river. Birds such as great blue herons, kingfishers, trumpeter swans, and Canada geese live, feed, and breed in the area.

The river's wildlife is protected in preserves alongside the river,

Below: *A grizzly bear feeds on leaves in a mountain forest.*

including Yellowstone and Grand Teton National Parks in Wyoming. South of the Teton Range is the National Elk Refuge, home to ten thousand deer, including many endangered elk.

Eagle Country

As the Snake flows out of the mountains onto the Snake River Plain, the wildlife living beside it changes. The thick forest gives way to more open land, and animals such as jackrabbits and pronghorn antelope are more common. Where the river broadens into reservoirs, waterbirds such as white pelicans, ducks, and geese become more common, especially during migration seasons.

As the Snake River Plain meets the Columbia Plateau, the river runs through the Snake River Birds of Prey National Conservation Area. There, sheer cliffs loom over the river, providing nest sites for many types of birds of prey. Prairie falcons, northern harriers, and golden eagles all live in the protected zone, feeding on the communities of squirrels and gophers, which inhabit the deep soils at the top of the canyons. Badgers also feed on these little animals. Badgers are more common in this refuge than almost anywhere else in North America.

Canyon Wildlife

Farther north, the Snake River passes through Hells Canyon, where wild sheep and goats are common. Black bears, mountain lions, and bobcats all hunt here, and everything from grouse to elk is on the menu. River fish in Hells Canyon include steelhead salmon, catfish, and smallmouth bass. There are also giant white sturgeons. These fish are now very rare, but at 12 feet (3.5 m) long and weighing more than 1,000 pounds (450 kilograms), white sturgeons are the river's largest fish.

Below: *A white pelican rests after feeding. The bird's long beak has a baglike sac under it, which the bird uses to carry fish it scoops up from river water.*

DAM BUSTERS

One hundred years ago, the Snake River was brimming with salmon. Every year, millions of coho, chinook, sockeye, and steelhead salmon traveled up the river to breed. The fish can recognize the smell of the streams where they hatched, and they sniff out the same stream when it is time for them to breed. Today, coho salmon are extinct in the Snake River.

The reason for lower numbers of fish is the dams on the Columbia and Snake Rivers, which block the migrating routes of the salmon. Millions of dollars are being spent every year to transport young salmon downstream past the dams in barges. Artificial concrete rapids—salmon ladders—provide a route back upstream for adult fish returning to breed. Unfortunately, these programs do not seem to be working as well as hoped because many of the salmon still cannot find their way to their home streams.

Above: *Water tumbles down the stepped salmon ladder at Ice Harbor Dam in Washington.*

Above: *A salmon ladder provides a route for migrating fish to travel over high river dams.*

3 Exploring New Lands

Lewis and Clark were the first U.S. explorers to marvel at the beauty of the Snake River. Since that time, the river has witnessed the coming and going of many different people.

Below:

Sacagawea, a Shoshone, helps explorers Lewis and Clark on their journey to the Pacific.

The first people to live alongside the Snake River were hunters descended from the people who had traveled from Siberia to Alaska about 14,000 years ago. They reached the Rocky Mountains about 8000 B.C., and evidence of their lives can still be seen today. In Wyoming, for example, there are the remains of prehistoric quartzite quarries. Quartzite was a type of rock used to make spear tips and arrowheads.

Native Ancestors

The Snake River's Native peoples are descended from the ancients who used these quarries. The land along the Snake's course in Wyoming and southern Idaho was once home to the Shoshone people. Farther north and west, the Snake ran through the territory of the Nez Perce people. This name is a result of their practice of wearing bones through their noses (*nez percé* means "pierced nose" in French). The Nez Perce also lived in the valleys of the Salmon and Clearwater Rivers.

Both the Shoshone and Nez Perce moved with the seasons, following the

movements of the animals that they hunted. The Nez Perce traveled between settlements, which they built alongside the Snake and its tributaries. Each village had a central longhouse, which was used for ceremonial purposes in summer and for shelter in winter. These buildings were more than 100 feet (30 m) long and were lived in by several families at a time.

The Shoshone lived in tepees and traveled more widely. After the arrival of Europeans, the Shoshone used horses and guns and became increasingly hostile to newcomers. They became skilled riders, and their territory ranged from their early homelands along the Snake River all the way to the Great Plains to the east.

Today, most Shoshone people live in western Wyoming. Others still live alongside the Snake River, in the Fort Hall Reservation of southern Idaho. The Nez Perce Reservation straddles the Clearwater River just east of Lewiston, Idaho.

Above: *A picture of Shoshone hunters painted on a bison hide from 1875.*

Below: *Petroglyphs on a boulder in Hells Canyon, Idaho.*

SET IN STONE

Traces of the nation's earliest inhabitants can be seen in many places along the Snake River. Petroglyphs (rock etchings) and pictographs (rock paintings) appear in a number of sites. They are particularly common in Hells Canyon and the Snake River Birds of Prey National Conservation Area. Most of the rock art left by early Native Americans shows strange peoplelike figures, some with horns and many carrying objects that look like weapons.

American Explorers

In 1800, the Snake River was known only to Native people. Within a few years, all that would change. In 1803, President Thomas Jefferson ordered a secret meeting to arrange an expedition to find a route from the east to the Pacific Ocean. The meeting was kept secret because at that time, the land west of the Rocky Mountains belonged to the British. Jefferson chose his young friend Meriwether Lewis to lead the expedition. Lewis picked an experienced frontiersman, William Clark, to join him as coleader.

Lewis and Clark's journey began in May of 1804. By September 1805, with help from a Shoshone woman, Sacagawea, they had reached what is now northern Idaho. The explorers were half-starved by the time they came down from the mountains onto a prairie near present-day Weippe, Idaho. There, they met a Nez Perce chief named Twisted Hair, who offered them food and led the expedition down the Clearwater River to the Snake. He made them canoes and at one point helped save members of the party from drowning after one of the canoes hit a rock.

Below: *Pioneers drive their cattle along the Oregon Trail in Wyoming, heading for the Snake River.*

NAMED IN HONOR

Where the Clearwater River meets the Snake River are the cities of Clarkston and Lewiston. These cities are named in honor of the two U.S. explorers who first saw the land, on which the cities are located. Each city has grown from a small collection of farms into a thriving industrial center. Lewiston was Idaho's first capital, before passing the title to Boise in 1864. Clarkston, on the west bank of the Snake River, is Washington state's most eastern city.

Right: *A view of Lewiston, Idaho, across the Snake River from Clarkston, Washington.*

Lewis and Clark reached the Snake River on October 10, 1805, making camp across the river from where Clarkston, Washington, stands today. Their journey down the Snake to the Columbia River took less than a week.

Rich and Poor

In 1810, U.S. businessman John Jacob Astor, the world's richest man at the time, decided to search for an easier path to the Pacific than the one that Lewis and Clark had taken. His idea was to follow the entire course of the Snake River to the Columbia. Astor sent a party of men to test the route, but things did not go

JUMPING THE RIVER

In 1974, Evel Knievel, the motorcycle daredevil, tried to jump nearly one-third of a mile (0.5 km) across the Snake River Canyon, just upstream from Shoshone Falls near Perrine Bridge, Idaho. He used his Skycycle, a rocket-powered motorbike with wings, for the stunt. He took off at 125 miles per hour (200 kph) from a ramp on the south rim of the steep river canyon, reaching 350 mph (560 kph) as he soared across the chasm. Once he was above the northern rim of the canyon, Knievel ejected and parachuted toward the ground. However, winds blew him into the canyon, and he narrowly avoided landing in the river.

Left: *Evel Knievel's steam-powered rocket bike blasts off during his failed attempt to jump over the Snake River Canyon.*

Below: *A large gold-refining machine near Idaho Falls, Idaho, uses river water to separate particles of gold from crushed rock and soil in the early twentieth century.*

well. At Caldron Linn in Idaho, one of the canoes was smashed by the rapids, killing one man and destroying much of the expedition's supplies. Later, the party found the Snake became even more wild and decided that it was not possible to navigate. There was no easy water route to the Pacific Ocean.

Mountain Men

For the next twenty years, the only people to come to the Snake River Valley were mountain men. Mountain men lived tough and lonely lives out in the open. They survived by hunting beavers and selling the furs to traders. A mountain man called John Colter came across what is now known as Yellowstone, but nobody believed his tales of a land

where mud bubbled and water shot straight up into the air.

A Long Journey

As beaver fur became less popular in the 1830s, many of the mountain men became farmers. Others led wagon trains of pioneers along a new land route to the Pacific—the Oregon Trail. In the area that became Idaho, the Oregon Trail largely followed the Snake River. Fort Hall was an important stop. Built in 1834 as a trading post for beaver fur, the fort soon found itself sheltering more pioneers than trappers. From Fort Hall, the pioneers followed the trail along the south side of the river. At Three Island Crossing near the present-day town of Glenns Ferry, the pioneers

Above: *Bars and cafés in the Basque Block area of Boise, Idaho. The streets are decorated with Basque flags.*

were forced to make a tough decision. They could either try to cross to the north side of the Snake for a direct route to the next stop, Fort Boise (near Idaho's present capital city of Boise), or they could continue on the south side and make the longer, but safer journey around the river bend. About half attempted the difficult crossing, using the islands as stepping stones. Not everyone made it to the other side of the river.

Fort Boise, like Fort Hall, was a trading post for beaver skins. Once the pioneers left there, they also left the course of the Snake River as the Oregon Trail continued through the Blue Mountains into Oregon.

Lucky Strike

In the 1850s, gold and silver were discovered in the mountains around the Snake River. As the news spread, people began to crowd into the area from all over the world, all hoping to strike it rich. Near the largest mines, towns grew up almost overnight, only to be deserted a few years later as the mines were exhausted.

Many of the unemployed miners moved to the newly built Boise City, which had been constructed to replace

THE STORY OF A BOOMTOWN

A few miles from the Snake River in southern Idaho lies Silver City (below). Today, it is a ghost town, but in the 1860s, its residents were the richest people in the state. Between them, Silver City's twenty-five hundred miners dug out sixty million dollars worth of gold and silver.

Silver City may have been rich, but it was also very rowdy. There were often conflicts among mine owners. In 1868, two separate mines found themselves working the same seam. When their tunnels met underground, there was a gunfight over who owned the gold. One man was killed, and although a truce was negotiated, the competing mine owners later shot each other dead on the porch of the town hotel.

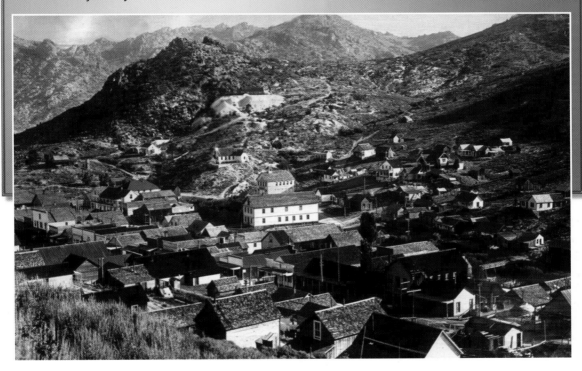

the derelict Fort Boise 50 miles (80 km) to the west. As well as being home to many descendants of Chinese gold miners, present-day Boise has the largest Basque community in North America. Boise's Basques are related to shepherds who moved to the area from their homes in northern Spain and southern France.

At the start of the twentieth century, the taming of the Snake River began. Dams were built, allowing the construction of large-scale irrigation projects. The fertile soils proved perfect for growing crops such as wheat and potatoes. During World War I (1914–1918), the region's farmers supplied food to Europe.

4 The Frontier River

The mighty current of the Snake River supplies the people of Idaho with electrical power and water for cities and farms. Thanks to the river, Idaho is now a thriving center of food production.

Like most of the United States' rivers, the Snake River is no longer the tumbling, untamed torrent it once was. While some of the river remains wild and beautiful, much of it is now controlled by dams, making it a calm and deep channel.

Calming Whitewater

The first dam on the Snake's course is Palisades Dam just inside Idaho's eastern border. Behind it, the huge Palisades Reservoir backs up into Wyoming. This lake supplies both states with water, used in cities and on farms, and the dam uses the river's current to generate electricity.

Farther into Idaho, the Snake River is held back by the American Falls Dam. Like the Palisades Dam, the American Falls Dam was built to create a reservoir of water to be used by people,

Left: *Water jets out of Brownlee Dam near Hells Canyon.*

On June 5, 1976, four years of work and the lives of eleven people were washed away in a terrible disaster. Teton Dam was a 305-foot- (192-m-) high bank of earth and rock across the Teton River, a tributary of the Snake, in eastern Idaho. The dam, near Rexburg, collapsed as the lake behind it was being filled for the first time. The reservoir had reached 17 miles (27 km) upstream, but it took just five hours to empty. The wall of water that roared downstream drowned 16,000 cattle and flooded the homes of 25,000 people.

Right: *Water cascades through the collapsed Teton Dam.*

A skier takes to the air while skiing down a steep mountain slope near Jackson Hole in the Grand Tetons.

as well as to generate electricity. The American Falls Reservoir is the largest on the Snake River and a popular destination for bird-watchers, fishers, and water sports enthusiasts.

Water Power

Milner Dam, 75 miles (120 km) downstream from American Falls, is the newest dam across the river. Rebuilt in 1992 on the site of an older dam, it is used mainly for power production. Milner Dam is located in an area popular with kayakers and whitewater rafters. Just below the dam is a narrow gorge. On a few days each year, water is released from behind the dam to pour through the gorge. Kayakers and rafters enjoy running the temporary rapids created.

Past Milner are the power plants at Twin Falls. For much of the year, the water flow over Shoshone and Twin Falls is reduced because water is taken out of the river farther upstream. The best time to see the falls is in spring, when water from melting mountain snow swells the Snake River and thunders down the course the way it did before the dams were built.

Power Museum

Three more power plants straddle the river before the town of Kuna, Idaho. The oldest power plant on the Snake River—Swan Falls— is also near there. Built in 1901 to supply electricity to the now deserted Silver City, the original plant at Swan Falls is now a museum. A new powerhouse took its place in 1994.

Where it forms the border between Idaho and Oregon, the Snake River has cut Hells Canyon. As it runs through the canyon, the Snake encounters three dams: Brownlee, Oxbow, and Hells Canyon. All three were built for making

FRIES TO GO

Idaho is famous for growing potatoes, and nearly all of its potatoes are grown along the Snake River. The fertile land is irrigated by water taken from the river and fed into the soil using networks of pipes and sprinklers.

Many of Idaho's potatoes end up as fries (below) in fast food restaurants. About a third of all the potatoes eaten in the United States come from Idaho, and the industry generates $2.5 billion every year—15 percent of the state's income.

electricity. The reservoir behind Brownlee Dam is the longest on the Snake, stretching back 57 miles (91 km). In Washington State, there are four more dams across the Snake.

Thirsty Crops

Agriculture along the Snake has a long history, and the river is a lifeline to thousands of farmers. Farmers who grow crops have particularly close ties to the river. More than 5,100 square miles (13,210 sq km) of crop land

Far right:
Vacationers paddle through some of the Snake River's beautiful surroundings.

in Idaho, for example, are irrigated by water from the Snake River. Farmers there grow potatoes, wheat, sugar beets, alfalfa fodder, bluegrass, hops for beer, and mint. Without the river water, all of those crops would die, and the farmers would go out of business.

The irrigation projects that run from the Snake are mainly concentrated in Idaho. Most have been in place for about one hundred years, and while they have helped farmers, they have also caused a huge drop in the number of salmon in the Snake. The dams prevent the salmon from swimming upstream to their breeding grounds. The battle for river water is not a simple one, and everyone cannot have all the water they want.

Most farms near the Snake River grow crops, but that is not all that is produced in the area. The Snake River Plain in southern Idaho has many dairy farms, producing milk, cheese, and butter, and herds of beef cattle and flocks of sheep graze near the river.

River Trade

As well as providing water to feed animals and crops, the Snake River has another role for farmers. From Lewiston to Pasco, the Snake is wide enough to be

Above: *A barge enters the lock at Ice Harbor Dam on the Snake River in Washington. The lock will raise the barge to the same level as water on the other side of the dam.*

used by large barges. Farmers in eastern Washington use the barges as an inexpensive way to transport grain.

Life in the Snake River Valley, however, is about more than power generation and farming. Most people in the area live in cities such as Lewiston and Boise and make their money in various industries. More people in the region work in factories than any other type of industry. The area's factories make electrical products and manufacture wooden items. Others pack meat and process vegetables grown in the region.

The states near the Snake River receive large amounts of their income from natural resources. Mining was a boom industry one hundred years ago, and it still employs many people today. The region's mountains are rich in silver, phosphates (used to make chemicals), and the metal molybdenum (used in steel production). Many other people in the region work for lumber companies, harvesting timber from mountain forests.

Natural Wonders

Another important industry, and one that is growing all the time, is tourism. The scenery along the Snake River draws people from all over the world. Yellowstone and Grand Teton National Parks are among the most visited in the country, and every winter, skiers flock to mountain resorts such as Driggs and Jackson Hole.

The Snake River is a draw for nature lovers and adventure seekers of all kinds. It offers opportunities for everything from water-skiing to whitewater rafting.

Tourism supports a wide range of businesses. Shops, restaurants, and hotels all thrive on the vacation money brought into the area by people from across the country and around the world. Some towns along the Snake, particularly those near resorts, make virtually all of their money from tourism.

Right: *A father and son try to catch trout in Henry's Fork, using a fishing technique called fly-fishing, in which an artificial fly is cast and dragged across the water's surface.*

FISHING AT HENRY'S FORK

Flowing 60 miles (96 km) from hot springs in the mountains down to the Snake River Plain, Henry's Fork in southeastern Idaho is considered to be one of the best fly-fishing rivers in the United States. Filled with rainbow and Yellowstone cutthroat trout, this tributary of the Snake River attracts fishers from far and wide. Many come for the scenery as well as the fishing. Henry's Fork is fed by warm springs and flows through a pristine wilderness of meadows and open forests, which are home to moose, elk, beavers, and sandhill cranes.

5 Places to Visit

The Snake River and its surroundings offer a host of attractions for visitors. The wonders of nature are never far way, and the area contains several historic sites.

❶ Old Faithful, Yellowstone National Park, Wyoming
The world's most famous geyser, Old Faithful (left) bursts into life every seventy-eight minutes, shooting boiling hot water 180 feet (55 m) into the air over Yellowstone National Park.

❷ St. Anthony Sand Dunes, Idaho
This 35-mile (56-km) stretch of rolling sand dunes is a few miles north of Henry's Fork. The 300-foot (91-m)

WASHINGTON

❿ Pasco

IDAHO

MONTANA

Hells Canyon

Heaven's Gate Lookout

❾

Oregon ❽
Trail Museum

Salmon River Canyon

OREGON

❼ Old Fort Boise Park

❻ Birds of Prey Conservation Area

St. Anthony Sand Dunes

❷

Yellowstone National Park

❶ Old Faithful

❸
Craters of the Moon National Park

❺
Hagerman Fossil Beds

❹ Shoshone Falls

Snake River

WYOMING

dunes (below) are popular with sand buggy enthusiasts in summer and snowmobilers in winter.

❸ Craters of the Moon National Park, Idaho
This park contains a huge lava field filled with hundreds of volcanic formations, such as cones and lava tubes. At first, the area appears to be barren and lifeless—hence its name—but visitors to the park will see a surprising amount of wildlife in this unusual landscape.

❹ Shoshone Falls, Idaho
Known as "The Niagara of the West," Shoshone Falls plunge 212 feet (65 m) as the Snake River thunders down toward the Columbia Plateau. The falls are at their wildest in the spring, when meltwater from the mountains swells the Snake River's flow.

❺ Hagerman Fossil Beds National Monument, Idaho
The Hagerman Fossil Beds paint a picture of life before the last ice age. Animals that lived and died there three and a half million years ago, such as mastodons and saber-toothed cats, are preserved as perfect fossil skeletons in the exposed rocks.

❻ Snake River Birds of Prey National Conservation Area, Idaho
More birds of prey nest here than anywhere else in North America. There is more to the National Conservation Area than just bird-watching, however. Visitors can get involved in everything from fishing to mountain biking.

❼ Old Fort Boise Park, Idaho
An exact copy of the original Fort Boise trading post, which was founded in the area in 1834, has been built beside the highway. The fort also contains a restored pioneer's cabin. Every year, the people of Parma celebrate their history on Old Fort Boise Day.

❽ Oregon Trail Museum, Oregon
Visitors can imagine life on the Oregon Trail at this fantastic museum with original artifacts from some of the trailblazers who passed though the area 150 years ago. Five miles (8 km) to the east is the National Historic Oregon Trail Interpretive Center, which adds to the experience with films and detailed displays.

❾ Heaven's Gate Lookout, Idaho
At 8,429 feet (2,569 m), Heaven's Gate Lookout overlooks the two deepest gorges in North America, Hells Canyon—the deepest—and the Salmon River Canyon to its east.

❿ Pasco, Washington
Built where the Snake, Columbia, and Yakima Rivers meet, Pasco is a small but thriving city set amid irrigated farmland. As well as its own attractions, the city provides a great base from which to visit the nearby Sacagawea State Park.

Above: *The Inter City Bridge crosses the Columbia River at Pasco.*

How Rivers Form

Rivers have many features that are constantly changing in shape. The illustration below shows how these features are created.

Rivers flow from mountains to oceans, receiving water from rain, melting snow, and underground springs. Rivers collect their water from an area called the river basin. High mountain ridges form the divides between river basins.

Tributaries join the main river at places called confluences. Rivers flow down steep mountain slopes quickly but slow as they near the ocean and gather more water. Slow rivers have many meanders (wide turns) and often change course.

Near the mouth, levees (piles of mud) build up on the banks. The levees stop water from draining into the river, creating areas of swamp.

❶ **Glacier:** An ice mass that melts into river water.

❷ **Lake:** The source of many rivers; may be fed by springs or precipitation.

❸ **Rapids:** Shallow water that flows quickly.

❹ **Waterfall:** Formed when a river wears away softer rock, making a step in the riverbed.

❺ **Canyon:** Formed when a river cuts a channel through rock.

❻ **Floodplain:** A place where rivers often flood flat areas, depositing mud.

❼ **Oxbow lake:** River bend cut off when a river changes course, leaving water behind.

❽ **Estuary:** River mouth where river and ocean water mix together.

❾ **Delta:** Triangular river mouth created when mud islands form, splitting the flow into several channels called distributaries.

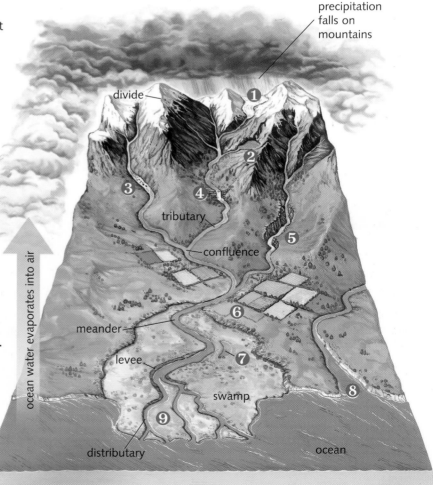

precipitation falls on mountains

divide

tributary

confluence

meander

levee

swamp

distributary

ocean

ocean water evaporates into air

Glossary

agriculture The practice of growing crops and raising livestock as an industry.

basin The area drained by a river and its tributaries.

canal A man-made waterway used for navigation or irrigation.

cargo Transported products or merchandise.

confluence The place where rivers meet.

conservation Protection of natural resources and the environment.

dam A constructed barrier across a river that controls the flow of water.

freshwater Inland water that is not salty.

gorge A narrow, steep-sided valley or canyon.

habitat The place where animals and plants naturally live.

industry Producing things or providing services in order to earn money.

irrigation Watering crops with water from a river, lake, or other source.

migration A regular journey undertaken by a group of animals from one climate to another for feeding and breeding purposes.

navigate To travel through water, steering in an attempt to avoid obstacles.

reservoir An artificial lake where water is stored for later use.

source The place where a river begins.

tributary A river that flows into a larger river at a confluence.

valley A hollow channel cut by a river, usually between ranges of hills or mountains.

For Further Information

Books

Harward, Lanny. *Snake River Secrets.* Frank Amato Publications, 1996.

Katschke, Judy. *Snake River.* Raintree/Steck-Vaughn, 1998.

Swinbarne, Stephen, R. *Once a Wolf: How Wildlife Biologists Fought to Bring Back the Gray Wolf.* Houghton Mifflin, 1999.

Wilkinson, Todd. *Yellowstone and Grand Teton National Parks.* NorthWord Press, 1999.

Web Sites

Grand Teton National Park
www.nps.gov/grte

Birds of Prey National Conservation Area
www.id.blm.gov/bopnca

Special Places: A Guide to Exceptional Features on Idaho's Public Lands
www.id.blm.gov/spec_places/index.htm

Yellowstone National Park
www.nps.gov/yell

Index

DATE DUE

FOLLETT